OWNING THE NOT SO DISTANT WORLD

Poems

by

Grace Cavalieri

BLUE LIGHT PRESS ◆ 1ST WORLD PUBLISHING

SAN FRANCISCO ◆ FAIRFIELD ◆ DELHI

Owning The Not So Distant World

1st World Library
PO Box 2211
Fairfield, IA 52556
www.1stworldpublishing.com

Blue Light Press
www.bluelightpress.com
bluelightpress@aol.com

Book & Cover Design
Melanie Gendron
melaniegendron999@gmail.com

Cover Art
Cosmos by Grace Cavalieri

Author Photo
Sandy Jackson Cohen

First Edition

Library of Congress Cataloging-in-Publication Data

ISBN: 978-1-4218-3561-7

DEDICATED

To my daughters: Cynthia Ann, Colleen Patricia,
Shelley Anne, Angela Beth

Owning The Not So Distant World

Contents

Whether By Good Or Bad Fortune

House

Within the wall there is
a room
and in the room
there is a
chair and
on that chair
there sat a man
and in that
man there was
a home made
of woman
chair and wall
and on that wall
there is a photo and
in that photo there
smiles a man and
on the rug there
sat the chair
and in that chair
a woman came
and took the hand
of the man who in
the photo held
a woman's hand and
to that wall they
both assembled
to stand within
a golden frame
until the day

this poem was
written so
they could
sit upon a chair
within the walls
where there was
once a rug and
where there
was a chair
with a man who
loved a woman
who loved a man
who held his hand
within a house
made of walls.

White Suit

I always loved one and so when Ken came back from
Australia

I bought a crisp linen suit just to greet him wearing white
spectator pumps red toes and heels

they don't make them anymore

and a polka dot blouse red and white dots with a bow though
now I wonder if it was such a good idea

he was 19 and I was 17 and he'd been gone 18 long months
with letters so passionate it took weeks to get one so much
loving and longing in two letters a day triple on Sunday

he was traveling alone staying at the Stacy Trent hotel in
Trenton

but I didn't know how to drive so I took the bus uptown to
Stuyvesant Avenue slow as a caterpillar caught in a traffic
jam turning right onto Prospect then left to West State
smoothing my skirt counting the trees

finally up to his floor stopping to see each number hoping to
appear as a clandestine lover until he opened the door
nothing was planned how could it be we looked at each other
and neither of us knew quite what to do he said Hi I said Hi
then he said Hi and I said Hi

We should have flung into each other's arms acting out all those words all those letters but without the emotional wherewithal it was a dam that could not break

catatonic for seconds then finally some talk we noticed the beautiful furniture in such an expensive room the silken drapes the sculptured pots

We even mentioned the light the weather but after that what else to say so I left and took the bus back home

I hung my white suit carefully in the closet wrapped the shoes back in plastic and reached into the drawer for his beautiful large packet of letters.

1937

We called them hobos, then,
one by one, coming to our back door.
God knows it was modest enough –
what they passed –
clothes freezing on the line,
wooden steps near the cellar.
Always to the back, they came,
I guess nearer the tracks,
or maybe because a woman
most likely would open there.
Of course these men were dirty,
unshaven,
some wore dented hats, some
kerchiefs around their throats.
I'm not sure if my mother ever told my father.
She would walk through the pantry
past the sewing machine, the clutter,
dried bread stacked for stuffing,
rag rug rolled up in the corner, she walked through
to open the door and close it again,
said Wait Here,
then brought out the yellow dish
painted with a single pink rose.
It was one of a kind, the rest had been broken,
leaving this on the top shelf.
This was her pride, she couldn't bear
to risk the kitchen wear. I would wonder
how it seemed
to them, outside, looking at the room into the kitchen,

wet woolen snow suits,
yellow linoleum floor, boots,
an ironing board. I bet they wished
it was theirs. My mother would come back
with food high on the plate
to stand behind
the closed door 'till they knocked and said
they were through
and thank you and then they went away,
until the next one would come, some other day.
I wondered if they thought the yellow plate
was pretty, probably from a full set
with other dishes, feeding our family around
a clean table every night, with napkins.
I often thought:
did any of them –
once they finished eating –
look at the yellow plate with its rose
unfolding at the center
know it was
just for poor people.
At five, I felt my face flush with shame –
I hoped they didn't know it was the only one.

To Judy

How the furniture in the house must have mourned love's absence

How heavily we sat on our mother's crushed red velvet couch

How from darkness I created you to be my darling, my duckling, my playmate

How things got away from us like a book underlined in the wrong places

How we always chose the worst of mud which never grew a Lotus

How my eyes burned for meanings as we became hollow puppets

How frightening the difficult tunnel we could not enter, the time we could not buy

How I wish justice would cultivate my heart as I search each memory

How the machinery of the day did not work or else there was a vocabulary we could not say

How either way your dying isn't exactly what I thought it would be

They Say Nothing Ever Dies

Past the great burst of jagged stars separating me from that (beautiful) day

From the dazzle of happiness that stays (sweetly) on my tongue

From the cold moon rising to (over) a future that's overrun

Like blooms on a stalk that never die (will not)

Lavish memory drifts into my (always) dreaming and

I am happy with the (remembered) notion:

Ken cooking eggs on a Coleman stove on the sand dunes of Florida

Where Cindy plays

And twin playpens are in the shallow end

So each two-year-old could splash
I am exploring the notion that it is still there somewhere.

Where could it have gone

All that beauty around us and in us. It has to be somewhere

Energy never goes away although I know (well I know) how perilous time's pistol can be

(Still) (yet) because I am (a fool, or brave, or) in pain with longing

I look back and wave and wave

I am waving and waving and I will, (I will) until someone waves back.

Message In The Drawer

Swoosh my white wedding gown trailing through time
swishing the velocity of my last fast dance the blur of love
gone right praying what is lost in the moment will soon be
found in my heart's vessel like birds flapping in the clock
tower now that you found me don't go away I believe and say
you are my alpha and omega and my delta and my vega but in
every hello is a goodbye even on Valentine's Day.

The Good Marriage

I said I'd always wanted to be at the water's edge
when dawn first lit the pink lake
so I could do Tai Chi in adagio
and chant with the world when birds were first waking
where grass would be wet with air between day and night
and there was this man I spoke to who set the alarm for
4 30 AM
not just to placate but to please
and hastened to fill the thermos with tea
and drove with me to witness the breath of beginning
while light was paused before fully lifting
and I'd always wanted to be at the water's edge
and I remember there was plenty of honey in the tea
and we witnessed the unfolding bouquet
a morning without velocity or dynamics or anything grand.

My French Neighbor, Renee

How Renee laughed at our American friend who divorced a
husband caught
kissing someone else's wife. "In France we look the other way"
she said –
her husband allowed to go away to Paris each summer to see
his Michelle.
"Remember Charles de Gaulle," she said, "his funeral with a
wife and mistress
side-by-side, civilized, enlightened, each his bride."

Then why, in her late life, did she show us letters slipped
under her door
signed "Michelle," her madness claiming she heard Michelle
walking
up her steps, Michelle carrying a light. How could Renee
know
that I saw her write the letters, herself, at night,
                                        signed
"Michelle."

Resume

We sit huddled in the hut waiting to see who will get the job

I have a Masters but nothing in the Classics

I wear a sparkling red shirt over my naked top anyway

You can't see through

Maybe my mother-in-law will rise from the dead

To give my dead sister her square diamond

And then give her approval for me to marry my dead husband

Then I wouldn't have to work

And he could build the neighbor's deck he always wanted as if he were 20 again

I don't really want that job or any other and I hope my friend will get it

He needs the money and I love to serve Iced tea

In The Beginning

all frippery and yellow cars
wide skirts   laughing and lace winging
through the forest   We thought spider webs were real
and took
to living in them
huddled bliss against the green
sometimes howling nights   then
Violets popped! Through winter's crust and from
our taciturn frost
and ashen wind
The Sun!
This is what we'd waited for all along
until
you dared   the path away
adventurer that you are
          leaving me alone in all this light

Watching From A Distance

where each day was a daughter carried like a leaf
everyone carved and touched
into shape to her own fortune
what is done is done
the candle burns low in the library
and what do you suppose those steadfast books
lined up on the shelf illustrate then
they speak of whatever loss is drying in the sun
nothing more
the fullness of the blessing once it leaves
the fulfillment of those gone to their own lives
and across the bridge into the other field
what do you think people are whispering
into the ears of horses
what do you think they're saying then
they warn of the forest as we walk slowly beside the locust trees
so many spikes you can find your way in the dark.

Crooked Pond

The poet acts as if her thoughts
are good enough and
indeed they are.
They are hers,
aren't they?

When she said them aloud
the important man
swore she was not talking
and swore it to his death.

They shared their love in common
and a grief
hammered by change,

but all those thoughts she had
she has no more
and no one ever heard them.

Simple Acts

It was getting in a hot car
and driving up the bright street
turning left

I think it was the thought of
cooking a turkey for the family

and the children looking friendly
climbing off the school bus

It was coffee by the pool
a long red dress
the plans for a wedding

It was the bird staying still on the
branch long enough to see.

Heart Mission

It wasn't so much that you were hurt –
And who among us is not hurt –
It's more that you had no one to tell,
I'm listening and
If loneliness still fits, wear it, let it cling,
If not, discard that jacket
And let me hold its warmth inside
Along with your forgotten treasures.

The muse chases all we love,
Didn't you know
It's a fountain of light
Where you burrow like a spy
Yet is always where we know you best.

Someday we'll find what was never seen,
Not by the book left open
Or the candle burned
The bell rung
But some song between us
Where people construct memories
Before the dream is done.

So sit with me
While bread and tea are warm
For what would be the wonder
If we didn't touch at all –
There would be no stars allowed
And didn't I tell you, Hope is itself a star.

Crystal Ball

I saw you in the future holding another woman's baby.
I saw you talking to her.
You were making her happy –
You didn't know I was watching. Please
do not refuse this to say I'm overreacting.

In the past you gave a banquet just for me
inviting everyone I ever knew,
even Shirley Temple was there.
You thought of everything. I didn't lift a finger.

You had the broccoli and cauliflower shimmering
on each plate with a single slice of bread perfectly
designed with its spread
and more of everything in the kitchen.

Didn't you know it was never that I wanted?
I wanted to take you in my arms and love you to death.
I woke up hungry from that dinner. And now there is the future,
no denying it. I saw it distinctly in my bad dream.

I was on a trip lost in work writing on a cliff,
seven miles away from anyone and you were at home
with your new heart – and for this nightmare there is no defense.

The Bride

SORROW asked me to marry him – he knew I'd fallen for him long ago. SORROW said how much he'd given to my heart – threatening my narrative with truth – how he made me understand what I loved best – SORROW claimed he took the fragments inside me changing them to stars and tears – I could not go on without him – he said – his hard dry love is the only thing that kept more harm from me – he told me to let him take over – I said *how will I survive you when I have to leave my children*. Sorrow took me in his arms, and said, "That's my job."

Recreation

how many swimming pools did we swim in during our marriage the one carved out of a hillside in California the Olympic sized ones where you were a medalist how did we rectify planning and voyaging the whole country just to plunge into swimming pools that weren't our own some people go for a sojourn but we doggedly traveled just to descend beneath the chlorine blue with sun slashing across our backs remember Key West its terse palms and soft sunsets we swam every day for 30 days and according to my diary in 100 different pools in 40 different states what did we want to dismantle to dive in so deep and become one with the current and sometimes the tumult of fresh oceans oh truculent air that will not hold me I want to go back to the car with its picnic and the first place we'd search for in new cities I want to have it again nothing but water between us.

Navy Housing

I don't know why we bought that house with a hole
in the living room floor
it extended throughout the room like a long wound
where 20 feet below was
a cement cavern
I couldn't look at it and I hate
to think of it even now
you can only imagine how hard it was
keeping my babies safe while they learned to crawl
much less their playmates
when neighbors came
but I was vigilant and fast and strong
one day when two children were clutching the side of the hole
I flipped them right up to safety
without even hesitating because
my husband was outside with the men
they were always
building airplanes to keep us safe
oh yes there were martinis and guests
many guests
and cigarettes and crepe suzettes
and black dresses with spaghetti straps and Trini Lopez records
listen once after the squadron was away
I covered the hole in the floor
with a table
and put three sculptures on it pretending we were fine
and we were we really were
although once the table jiggled and I almost started to cry
The Navy took the squadron away a lot

the last time when he was in Italy
he packed his suitcase full of Italian ice cubes
to bring home to me to share
they never made it but the men did and
we were in love
and nobody ever died and there was
always the next house and the next house and the next
please don't think I'm complaining
I would do it all over again but we were young then
you had to be young.

Guilt By Association

Although dead,
Jan appeared last night
looking trim and well dressed.
I shook her hand, formally
for the dead have no feelings
and are bothered by
our animations.
She went toward the door,
looked back, then she left, closing it.
I thought she meant to stay
but she was walking through to tell us
she'd be waiting on the other side –
this was her way to say
the person I was with would be joining her soon.
I cannot remember who it was.
I strained my thoughts, to find him,
to warn him.
Who was that night companion I brought along
to stroll through a dream, as
company for me,
never knowing he'd get fingered by the dead.
Who was unlucky enough to be with me
to watch from my close distance,
blundering into my dream like that
thinking innocently,
we were all enjoying the same thing at the same time.

Writing From The Clavicle

I tried to write a poem that wasn't from the heart

about the damage to my keyboard but the poem erased itself
from the page

not to speak of the fake hero I imagined (twice, that makes
two fake poems)

what a fool I was trying to get into *the New Yorker*

with words that turned from tears to marble on the page

realization came when my eyes would never open wide again

that's when I knew the uglies had taken me hostage

now in the evening of my life, I just *say it* and let the poem

be handyman for all that was broken and true.

Wedding Planner

For Ken

We said we had an inner knowing we
spoke of ascension awakening we
forgot suffering in the past we
turned memory into tenderness we
hurt each other into love we
did not judge this experience we
transmuted fear we
used our senses we
were awareness in action we
were kids afraid alone ready to make a new reality we
invented difference and sameness.

To Be Perfectly Honest With You

this poem didn't know it was dishonest –
thinking about small children
walking out from morning's mist
into the safe sun with me
warm and fed
never to sleep within sorrow –
I was writing about my own small children
I swear it –
while all the time another poem kept seeing
babies born in refugee camps
who become children
playing in the dirt with sticks and how
with winter's fire
there are no sticks –
that is the poem which wanted to be written
although it started with my own secret life
when suddenly –
a more daring poem broke the heart wide open
and this is the absolute truth.

Letter From Puerto Rico

If patience were a ray or sweet word
    It would never fail here
The keen bone of quiet is like faith
     Listen to the heat
     Feel the violet view
Cold motion has no reward
For Winter's just a painting on the wall
And Spring's wind is always perpendicular
     To time
Even if Lucille got the job you wanted
On the 5th floor with the Big Four
Shaking hands in her yellow suit
And chic bobbed hair
     She's dead now with unnarrowing
     Limits of grass
And the song succeeds with blackbirds
     And promise
Outlasting music's endnote.

Re-creation

On Wednesdays the nun visits the adult book shop
There's nothing she doesn't know about knees
She examines the testicular knobby males
And their heavy breasted females
She studies their farmyard behavior
On Wednesdays the nun visits the adult book shop
When she wore young dresses on a hill above the town
And met a boy who kissed her lips
Her soft skirt floating in the afternoon haze
On Wednesdays the nun visits the adult book shop
She walks the aisles to find the book
That shows what could have happened
The nun visits the adult book shop on Wednesdays
To find the page with the lilac breeze, the smell of honeysuckle

The Important Point I'd Like To Make Is

        His house was close to mine   right next
door   turn

left across their beautiful yard   to Mrs.
Levine   whose husband

carried   meat home   from their butcher shop   I'd
see Mr. L   bringing

    home   meat in white paper   every night at
5   their son

Bernie   the dentist   lived upstairs   close   dark curly
hair   quiet guy

he owed gold and cash to gamblers he had a
mystical plan   to pay

but the Mafia   wouldn't wait   his mother prayed and
begged for help

he died of nitrous oxide   by his own hand   in his
dentist's office
       I used to watch him from my sister's window
    when he was reading   or writing at his desk
an ordinary man

I think he had an older brother   I searched his name
his closest companion

I wish I could remember only three people would know
my mother father sister

    or   maybe Elaine Maskee down the street or Mrs
Milacci but they're gone

all gone like everyone else on the street
like the street.

Portrait Of A Lady Going To Heaven

Close Your eyes
Reflect on the horizon the absolute blue
Take your footprints off the earth and hurl them upward
Concentrate
Against running or jumping
That won't help
Wobble like a moth against reality
Never mind crawling up a cliff
Or fluttering out a 30-story building
Float harmony on air instead
Breathe faith instead of swallowing
Hemlock or plucking nightshade
Remember ordinary love
When he put his hand over yours
When you were afraid of an event
And he said
Don't Worry I'll Get You There.

Goodbye Dream

Goodbye to the three guys in plaid
shirts I hugged one by one who laughed
when my jokes were not funny
thanks for the way you pretended,
and to the old friend sleeping in my bed naked
and dead, goodbye, roommate.

And to the elderly gentleman who wanted to play
Chinese checkers, farewell, I was so
rude for three days I'm glad
you found another. You make a wonderful pair.

Now last night's dream is gone with its
walk in the woods where I stayed inside
– solo – watching you all in the rain.
I sat against the wall
clutching my grey, grey sweatshirt. I'm
glad to take it off.

Goodbye to all the books I owed the library,
the magazines I collected –
the stale munchies –
the constant cleaning up I did –
the ukulele contest across the street I refused –
Such a bad vacationer I am, on such a lonely vacation.

goodbye goodbye goodbye to the people
who could not make me happy.   I'm glad to go –
        Dream, why do I miss you.

Parity

For Maria Van Beuren

Not by sight but by faith I know he loves her still,
And I have sent myself here to tell you this.

Just when the seasons were failing and the snow had finally
begun,
the red finches arrived all at once to give us courage.

She was disinclined to believe a man could love her so
and she didn't believe the celebrity could last,

so I have sent myself here to tell you, he loves her still,
I know this not by sight but by faith.

In this late afternoon sun we ask what poetry remedies.
Nothing
at all, certainly not grief. Yet it does notice the radiance of
love.

It notices a doggie who sat up straight when Colin passed, a
doggie
who wagged his tail - a salute - small and definite.

Poetry notices Maria seeing Colin's spirit moved past her
saying,
"Why don't we go for a walk."

Poetry says every woman wishes she were able to wake next
to a man
in his last stage of life singing:

Let's talk dirty in Hawaiian, and singing the dirt as sweet
as a swan's breath.

It is not so much that loyalty can be measured like the sturdy
deck steps
he built, or the British bar he left for us, to raise him a toast.

It is more like this – a Parity. Maria was Colin's Angel of
survival.
And it was not what Colin FELT for Maria,

it was that he was capable of the feeling.
She could not believe her good luck. *He was capable of the
feeling.*

And with all the days that I have left
I'll think of that.

The Shakedown

With
this silver spoon
I tell the truth
I came
from a land
where love
was spare
parents better
off not paired
affection
stripped
to its essentials
a film I run
and can turn off
because
from a sea
of pure abundance
comes the trumpet
of happiness
sweeping me
into this place
more golden
than its birth.

Whether By Good Or Bad Fortune

A Green Thought About Yellow

Let's not make yellow heavy, for God's sake.
There's enough wrong in this world.

Take the Goldfinch. It's not how he looks but how he sounds,
bright with song that does not murmur apologies.
How you speak to me is everything, not only what you say.
Now, please do not be put off by this,
I'm trying to protect you from yourself and from me.
Were there times you did not feel anything?
When your ears were filled with snow?
Well, there will be times when you don't feel again.
That's a shame.
You see it is not your hard heart, I fear,
it is mine, if you turn back my love –

So let us have lunch in the upper room.
In my bright yellow and green caravan,
eat something predictable,
talking of the news,
holding this as keepsake between us,
although it may not be what you had in mind.

On My 90th Year

we knew from the beginning it was a glass factory refracting
shiny fragments into a version of the body but then
possibilities   there came music and prose
prose first like the wind
variance of sounds testing and breaking crystals   this was
the energy holding the mind
a rhythm of uncertainty   silence   speech that shaped this
sound
filaments of experience
tiny blue flowers on a teacup   the language of an artist
who is
always examining her work   always examining her
work
we took advantage of the fact that we were human   with
accommodations
pockets of imagery
the landscape it's always dangerous with desire   hot and dry
but cooler sailings promised
what would we surrender to get what we wanted
what moon would we reach   what natural mysteries
would enter   sometimes we sat
under a simple tree
where else was there to sit other times the habit of lighting up
the sky with red and blue festivity
do not think what I say here matters I'm trying to tell you the
shared recognitions that make us
in the world and free of the world at the same time
walking straight into water until we are
blind with it

and then what about whiteness what is pure and what is
vision
the impulse to make everything a dream   night   supper
noon   morning   its memory
now I see the wit and energy of it all the red carnations given
me the house on the hill the cemetery gleaming in its victory
I realize it's unnatural to talk about evenings   trips on
the ferry
a language of marriage looking for itself over and over   A
painting taking too long to finish
I am only saying   there stood a girl
alongside a green forest with no light no end
crystalline waterfalls   and she entered

Every Night In My Dreams Every Night We Are Back In The Navy Every Night

We are now in that big house on the water with so many levels.
The water splashes against the glass panes. We're just
settling in
when another family has nowhere to stay and is assigned to
us,
they can have that big room downstairs in the back,
a large bed, fresh sheets. Someone else just left –
The wife is from another country but speaks well. Her baby
has special needs and just stays silent in the crib or sleeping
on her shoulder.
We'll take them to a ride through the mountains to show
them Lunar Lake –
She's getting friendlier and talks about her baby, her fears,
when the driver goes around a barricade
errs on the right and almost makes it
then swerving, the car goes off down the cliff off the road's
edge –
We hang on to the top of the cliff with our hands and slowly
shimmy up using all our strength.
Athletic, we know how to pull up from the edge of swimming
pools
Once we're alive we feel good. Powerful. No one wept. She
feels what it is to have a superior mind and body
and how it is to be a Navy wife. Her hair starts to curl and
shine, she's fashionable.
She comes to parties with us where the bachelors, Navy
Ensigns,
live in lofts above theaters and read Simon de Beauvoir. She

tells stories in her broken accent about
being pregnant, the maelstrom of moving homes,
and hanging off a cliff. Everyone laughs and then goes off to
other parties.
I've made so many friends with so many women. We look into
each other's faces.
We blur. We'll never see each other again.
The best part of being in the Navy is this dream: My dead
husband and I decide where we want to retire. I want
that big house on a ring of water where the children were so
happy. He wants
that Alpine style in the mountains with a big workshop.
Every night the Navy gives us so many choices.

Whether By Good Or Bad Fortune

This is what remains
movement
at the top of the tree
gold and green branches in three parts
the middle like a dead bouquet
holding something at its space
where choice is made
and water goes sporadic to
its branch
that tells where storm has hit
the properties of movement
the constant turning points
reflecting what is left alive
between dead branches blowing
and add to that regret
the wrangled leaves
where death couldn't reach
the wind peaceful
spent as flame.

I Miss Romance

his language
   psychedelic hearts
 a full life
 blooming surprise
  forever loving soulful
 true and honest
 heart to words
    emotional core
  going big
with strength
 flawlessly executed
 this random love
 with rapture
 making possibilities
  and relatable moments
 ultimately to greater grandeur
   integrity of speech
   high in remembrance
 an even plane
and a good story
dynamic organic
solidifying foundational
   high-minded synergy
 with granular movement
 making a difference
  fountain of good
 aspirational ideation
 for phantom pleasure
  of a world less cruel

  dreaming
tomorrow's return
almost forgetting
all these words
 I inscribe them for the future.

Reversal

This poem can do whatever it wants –
It can change the past and make it new –
It can make hollyhocks bloom again
in my mother's yard,
pink and white against the wall where I sit
in the safety of summer mornings.
These words can take away the scarlet stab of blood
that entered my mother's brain
as she slept.   Here,
take this porcelain cup, blue and white,
and stir some memories for faces no longer seen,
then wander with me to pines that never grew,
to the cottage that was not there because this poem can
leap over any cold moon rising, over any landscape looming
to make this the happiest day of our lives.

Your Success Just Has To Catch Up With You

Wanting more of what you won't get
is a strange light to see by.
Close your eyes to time and eternity.
The world will still be here. All
the sheepskins hanging off the
mantel name your sins, a
rosary of shame. The only
excuse is that you didn't
know any better.
You join the war and find
life and death the same soldiers
on either side; no footprints
are left. No birds on the
branch. Your lover
glides up the driveway in a
pointy car the color of
your heart. The only trouble
is he's with his new girl.
You almost see a bluebird
near the box but it's
a leaf in shadow.
I guess there's no investment
but in going to your own garden,
stepping out of a raw river of coals
that gives no more light. Be
alone in your own house even if
upstairs they struggle
to continue the building. Surround
your spirit self. Enter the air fully

as an explorer who will plan
your own love after death.
Imagine a day with music and sunshine.
Now will be the peace
that passes understanding.
Will you meet me there?

Natural Accompaniments

When the sun gestures,
when the peaceful shaggy sun gestures
    over the mossy egg,
its sure lagging light falls
  over the myth
  over the mossy myth we travel
The shaggy myth becomes our egg

    Our travel gets peaceful
Egg: Are you really the sun
    on the road
breaking over the moss we travel
or, sun, are you the egg
breaking open upon us to wake us
    like gestures of light

Rewarded by other people's lives
a happiness we've never known
descends
    So this is what love is:
imagined, bolting, strong
This is the STRONG imagination
    bolting down happiness like
a wild bird healing us by
flying through other people's lives

And what of those others insulting
    the sky. The Zen say
Stop Thinking And Talking About It

And Then There Is Nothing
You Will Not Be Able To Know

So now we have a story – something
      we want to see together
      to talk of
in the coming of winter

The loneliness of ago

Through the silver of my eyelids –
by the sliver of your listening –

Reincarnation

When my eyes woke up from the amnesia of birth
I was lost in the river's contour
I was lost in the prairie's unbidden storms
I was running through the forest
The world seemed of no matter
It was all hunger   It was all motion

Our final day which begins today is not
what I looked for but for a moment it entered me
tangled in my flesh
It is present now
I knew suddenly what I wanted to tell you
about reanimation
There were names we belonged to
before we could see
haloed names that would become faces of family

I had lost my foothold and yet
for reasons I will never know
– from turmoil – suddenly light – seeming like joy
holding me like a perfect egg in a perfect hand and
I opened my life to this season of endings
and beginnings
trusting myriad tree and blossom   my only friends
which will be there after us
just as all is beautiful under the snow
If we do not understand this   what is there to understand?

Saga

Let's tell a story.
I'm safe within stories –
let's tell about the gifts I gave everyone
on my wedding day –
pearls shining fresh from an oyster's bed –
gold Clematis
crossed with the silver Japonica bush.

Let's make up some strawberries
hanging from the Willow tree.
Were they sweet enough for you?
And if I missed anyone, please no chiding,
this imagination outruns the clock –
If only my life had been later or earlier –
but never mind –
this must be seen as temporary –
a hastening breeze we'll soon forget.

Let's tell stories anyway,
about the hopes held that day,
peacocks flourishing, blue and red on our lawn,
goldfish tugging and gleaming, bright water,
white horses lazing in sun.

Otherwise, I promise,
our houses will have small windows
where we cannot see past hills –
blinded by buttressed rocks
hiding streams of every color
never seen before.

Instead let's talk about my line of vision,
creations of my own thinking,
where I can change stories with each hearing
before they'll fly off to time without me.

Your Awe Is Not My Awe

(overheard" The awe of battle")

My awe is a sacred space, a bird flying to the feeder
the shade of a tree
berries in the forest
not rockets of light.

My heat is from the sun
flames from memory switchbacked to experience
not the lashing of cannons.

My awe is the clear path of vision,
the razor straight edge of sky
a plumb where water is moved by stone.

How much has been lost: Mesopotamians, Babylonians,
Assyrians
tribal armies, monsoons, tsunamis
history shattered into pieces that will not fit together.

How large is loss? How much does it take to fill it?
How do we gather it in our arms?
After my children left there was a space I could not fill.
When cities were destroyed there is a space that will not fill.

Right now small children emerge hungry from sleep's groove.

My awe is the milk of the moon shining on these words
that come from me and will not return empty.

The Owl And The Pussy Cat

From the grave of old books
comes the best story ever told –
how on the trellis of the ocean
two creatures went to seek
their fortunes upon the
undulating sea –
Let us say jubilance and
bourbon were one as they
collapsed into their pea green
sieve sifting the foam
on its rise and collapse –
I love this story of feathers
and fur together without rancor
fearless and feckless just
as I was curled up then age three believing
every word of it – as in fact I do today.

A Hitchhiker In The Universe

As I meditate today and point my mind
like scissors diving into the darkness
many nomad thoughts intrude
people who need to be heard
and tasks that need to be done and as
I try to escape into my parallel world
to meditate
a voice comes saying
don't run away
this world of matter is part of that invisible world too
both are leaves forever birthing and unfolding
it's all the same
do not be ashamed of daily thoughts
this world is a part of the celestial
this chair may not know you
the house will not remember you but it is holy too
made of the same spirit as the planets
do not look away
as you meditate into the unknown haze
there is nothing more divine than anything else
and nothing will stay here
and yet will appear in the next world
carried over whether you believe it or not
leaving only your footprints shining on this sweet vanishing earth.

The Longest Story In The World

Phi Beta Kappa Ceremony
for Herman Ward
Trenton College of New Jersey

The longest story in the world is
Transformation

Sunrise to yellow
Rushing waters to waterfall
Seeds breaking earth
Birds' beaks breaking seed
All in service to the earth

Once 71 years ago
There was a professor
Who without having to say
Showed us how
To rinse off language
Study nature's magnificence
Notice everything
Slow down because
No one can dream in a hurry
Discover others
By finding out who we are
Animate imagination
Reread books and then write new ones
Tell everyone a poem
Make the world less lonely

For this is the heart's motion
And our deeds are all we can own

Sunrise to yellow
Rushing waters to waterfalls
Seeds breaking earth
Birds' beaks breaking seed.

A Statement Of Distance And Pieces

What could possibly be the function of an ocean
but to keep things apart, a cellophane

to make the water look real
it comes and goes only as vision will allow

like memory, for instance, that wizard of loss,
that stand-alone, presence-making, invasion

making us believe there's a connection to the past.
Love, like habit, dies hard, other times

evaporates incrementally with
disappointment but early on is like that

tangerine over there warming in the sun,
waiting to be undone cyclically,

peel by peel, with a taste never had before
like for the first time.

Haiku For The Turn Of The Year

The wolves with two lambs
The wolves with one lamb
The wolves

❁

Harvest light
Shadows long
Mothers always die

❁

At the columbarium
The bee
Buries itself
Inside the flower

❁

Points
On a map
Growing smaller now
Window porch street

❁

Scarlet Autumn
Purses lips
One last kiss

❁

Hoarfrost
On the wedding cake
Marriage over

✿

From the sky's
shorelines
All the stars fall out

The Fugitives

Under the expressive eye of the sun
An elephant

In this world with its upheavals and reversals
An elephant is killed

With a broad verified margin for error
An elephant is shot in the head

With an inability to love
An elephant is shot in the head 10 times

Profiting from greed, and weakness
An elephant has tusks ripped out

For not choosing the time well
An elephant wandered into range

For people who lost control of our past
An elephant is bleeding

For the ones who could not love or find love
A baby elephant is wandering lost

Lost At Sea

That Hart Crane's father
invented Life Savers candy
should not begin this poem
not funny and that he
died the year I was born
not relevant or funny
don't you wish you
knew what the sailor said
the one who rejected
him the night of Crane's
drunken prank standing
on that rail pretending
it was the East river. Don't
you wonder if he thought
of the insane guy in his
own poem who jumped off
the Brooklyn Bridge, that
moment, that exact moment
when he fell between the
crack of this world and the
next and was his last
thought of his beloved New
York with its neon lights,
soot, alleys and drains
as he plunged off a
coast of nothing but
cypress and Spanish
Moss, all that urban
legend from a
Mexican ship lost to a
flat Florida coast.

A History Of The World

Almonds and nuts grew the tallest trees
then there was man
and his arrow
death was invented
he walked wind-torn and thirsty
motion his only lesson
the sound of the owls
breaking night's glass
his only guide
what kingdom did this early man seek
what end did he wish for
they didn't know   these people
moving   always moving
along came translations
from animal sounds
they listened for a sharp break
in the leaves then named it
who among them
were the first ones who could speak
language came from their emptiness
from the table of wind came words
on time's horizon thoughts had wings
then speaking like rivers of sadness
cascading to sunrise flames
the fire of language failed
with all its beauty bestowed
the tongue was lost in confusion
retarding their love
men killed each other one by one
inside and outside the developing silence.

Owning The Not So Distant World

The stars come down to free creation from its bondage.
The sun is bathed in water
or is it the memory of a sky
in an evening illuminated by our eyes
which are illuminated by the evening.
Close them then
to see a little better.
All comfort does not belong to the outside world.
If we are dependent on that
we are dependent on
the tricks of the mind coming home,
attributing falseness to beauty,
thinking it will vanish,
when it has always just arrived.
An inner sight
is meant to keep us safe, saying our
names as if we were someone the world loves.

Fame

What is the part of your life
you can never forget?

Every part up to now?

The old man walked
out of the retirement home,

a shadow event:
that's him.

But what if everyone knew
his name – what then?
why he'd have nothing left to plan.

It was like the furniture he gave away
when his wife died.

In the back porch of his mind
he wondered what to let go of,
  – the word "of?"

Now no one in the home knew
where he was
and it'd take hours.

A woman near the lawn had on a crisp
White
Suit.

Trala
Removed a jacket, she did.
Under, was a bright
Green silk top.

She looked away.

What were the meaning of hands
if they could not touch?
But the sun shone on him anyway.
The sun didn't know its own name
yet it shone. Nice sun, that way.

Today was the day he would,
like Mozart, blinded by music and math,
find fame.

The ability to get to Heaven
is made of words,
not numbers. He tried to think of a word which
would get him there, probably a noun.

How did he feel?
It was the day after Christmas.
That's how.

A big sky, no trees.

Being so old. Like driving a car, when you
got out, still felt you were moving.
That kind of moving. All he had.

After giving up hitting girls,
little boys plucked bows from their
hair to prove
they got close.
He did that once. He was a boy like that.

A cat crossed.
People don't have yellow eyes
but that's all he could say for them,

Oh yes, Cat, you are just
a collection of thoughts
not suggestions. Better than people, that way.

What in your life would you let go of ... the "of?"

There are not enough things to think to
make you happy.
So thinking couldn't be it.

Where is the boy who walked down the hill?
Gone, he is gone.
And the husband who held babies in each arm,
Where is he?
He is gone.
And you old man, where are you going?
Away – away.

He whistled down the hill
and would pretend to be married
feeling something different everyday,

even the theft and the bruises.

Tell me it won't end this way,
loving
only what you
do not understand,
he told his hand.

When he felt bad, real bad, he knew
to go deeper and deeper.
There was something there he wanted. What?

Now he'd come to nothing after all.

A big elm
and the river.
Cold and wet, nice to feel.

Praise and blame were the same.
Didn't mean a damn at the end.

The hawk moved in circles,
tight circles gaining altitude.
Probably the heat of the road.

Birds and people's secrets died with them

To drink honey wine under a full moon.
Ah.
He knew the answer.
Honeymoon.

Even though someone wanted him to subtract
54 from 96, and he forgot.

Wrong to surprise a person
like that.
Not fair to ask him in front of the people.

Words are the way you get to heaven
not numbers, Stupid, he shouted, running out.

He'd be remembered for that. Oh yes. Remembered.

The drumming offbeat of the cars
on the road
made his heart skip around.
People should drive more evenly,
careful of people walking down the hill.

What was he trying to do?

He knew his birthday was in January
but the number of it...

well it was the difference
between owing and paying,
not there at all, empty
in his brain,
not there.

Where do numbers go, anyway?
And they shouldn't be used
to embarrass.

People mistook his quiet for thought
but it wasn't.

what was it? A story of silence?
He liked stories. They came from real pain

Real feeling

Let someone else
do your penance for you.
That's what stories do.

When his wife died he kept
one table
a purse
and a satin chair.

He could pay someone to say his name every day
or he could
leave them the chair,
probably no one would say your name
for a purse.

Here was the water. So cool. He could take off one shoe
then the other. Just like that.
A fine beginning.

"When is courage unnecessary?"
Once he taught the class.

It was a riddle he couldn't now
remember the answer to.

The river was wide
and he knew something about width –

that it wasn't the only measure
of rivers.
They could be deep
or they could not.
They were pretty because they went someplace.

Whatever we love shouldn't be kept
a big secret,
that's what he thought,
trying to make a list of all the nouns
which would keep him on earth
or move him up from it.

Someone would soon be talking
about him.
The name stolen from him would be free.
It'd be their worry now.

There in the far city a
crane did its work,
up and down.

If I'm not there
who'll get the chair.
He hummed a little tune to it and waded in.

All he ever wanted
was to give everyone he knew
a hundred dollar bill.

If a boat goes by,
I'll wave.

Then they'll recall
having seen me here.

He didn't understand why he thought like that.
His mind ran on fast
but unable, like water, to hold on,
sure that the angels would keep his birthday.

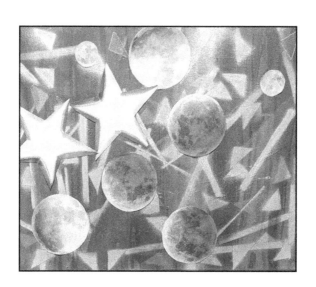

Acknowledgements

This book premieres poems, but for the following: "The White Suit" (*Foto Specchio & Best American Poetry*;)" "To Judy" (*Italian Americana*;) "The Good Marriage" (*Potomac Review*;) "Crystal Ball" (*Silk Road*;) "Letter From Puerto Rico" (*Plume*;) "Haiku For The Turn Of The Year" (*december*).

About Grace Cavalieri

Grace Cavalieri was Maryland's tenth Poet Laureate (2018-2024). She founded and still produces "The Poet and the Poem" for public radio, now from the Library of Congress, celebrating 47 years on-air in 2024. She holds two Allen Ginsberg Awards; The Paterson Award; the AWP George Garrett, Columbia, Bordighera, AAUW Awards; National Commission on Working Women Award, and the CPB Silver Medal, plus others. She's an Academy of American Poets Fellow. She's had 20 plays produced on American stages. In July 2023, twenty-five years of her podcasts were sent to the moon from NASA on Lunar Codex.

Books By Grace Cavalieri

Why I Cannot Take a Lover – (Washington Writer's Publishing House, 1975)

Body Fluids (Bunny and the Crocodile Press, 1976)

Swan Research (Word Works, 1979)

Bliss (Hillmunn Roberts Publishing, 1986)

Trenton (Belle Mead Press, 1990)

Migrations: Poems with Mary Ellen Long, art (Book Distribution, In Support, 1995)

Pinecrest Rest Haven (Word Works, 1998)

Heart on a Leash (Red Dragon Press, 1998)

Sit Down, Says Love (Argonne Hotel Press, 1999)

Cuffed Frays and Other Works (Argonne Press, 2001)

Greatest Hits, 1975-2000 (Pudding House Press, 2002)

What I Would Do For Love (Jacaranda Press, 2004)

Water On The Sun: Acqua Sul Sole (translated by Maria Enrico – Bordighera, Inc., 2006)

Anna Nicole: Poems (Goss 183: Casa Menendez, 2008)

Navy Wife (Goss 183: Casa Menendez, 2010)

Sounds Like Something I Would Say (Goss 183: Casa Menendez, 2010)

Millie's Sunshine Tiki Villas: A Novella in Verse (Goss 183: Casa Menendez, 2011)

Gotta Go Now (Goss 183: Casa Medendez, 2012)

Cosa farei per Amore: Poesie dalla voce di Mary Wollstonecraft (2013)

The Man Who Got Away (New Academia/Scarith, 2014)

The Mandate of Heaven (Bordighera Press, 2014)

Life Upon The Wicked Stage (New Academia/Scarith, 2015)

With (Somondoco Press, 2016)

Other Voices, Other Lives (Alan Squire Publishing, 2017)

Showboat (Goss Publications, 2019)

What The Psychic Said (Goss Publications, 2020)

The Secret Letters of Madame de Stael (Goss Publications, 2021)

Grace Art: Poetry and Paintings (Poet's Choice Publishing, 2021)

Why I Cannot Take A Lover, 2nd Edition (Washington Writer's
  Publishing House, 2022)

The Long Game; Poems Selected & New (The Word Works, 2024)

Owning The Not So Distant World (Blue Light Press, 2024)

Printed in the USA
CPSIA information can be obtained
at www.ICGtesting.com
LVHW051921210524
780968LV00009B/92